THE CEMETERY KEEPERS OF GETTYSBURG

LINDA OATMAN HIGH

ILLUSTRATIONS BY
LAURA FRANCESCA FILIPPUCCI

WALKER & COMPANY NEW YORK

I,
Fred Thorn,
son of the cemetery keeper,
was born in the gatehouse
near the gravestones
of Evergreen
Cemetery.

Papa was the caretaker:
digging graves,
pulling weeds,
keeping the grass green,
while Mama
took good care
of me.

When I
was just
a toddler,
my brother
George was
born,
then another brother
John was born
when I was
four.

We
loved
to play
our favorite
games
among
the graves
as Mama
planted
fragrant flowers
around
our gatehouse home,
sweetening
the air
around
Evergreen.

In the night,
I dreamed
of the bereaved,
and I believed
that
moon-white ghosts
floated
like kites
over the stones,
engraved with
names
of those
now gone
to a better
place.

It was a hot and
buggy
summer afternoon,
in August of 1862,
when Papa put on
a uniform of blue.

He was enlisting
in Company B
of the Pennsylvania
infantry.

"Don't cry," Papa said,
kissing us goodbye.
"I need to help the Union
fight the Rebs."

Mama was brave,
and gave Papa a hug,
but my brothers threw
themselves on the blue rug,
and wailed.

I promised Papa
that I wouldn't fail
to take care of Mama,
and I'd help her
tend the cemetery
while he was gone.

Papa was sent
to Virginia.
Mama grew large
with a baby—
maybe a sister
or another brother.

Our grandmother
and grandfather
with wrinkled skin
moved in
to live with us
because
Mama was
tired and dizzy,
busy and big.

Still, she strived
tirelessly
to dig the graves
of Evergreen,
with help
from me.

It was a Friday
in June, and I
was moping,
hoping
that soon
Papa would come home.

He'd been gone
for too long,
and I feared
he'd never return.

Churning butter,
I heard
sudden shouts
from all over town,
loud sounds
from guns,
and horses'
hooves pounding
the ground.

"Run! The Rebels are here!"
people screamed
as men
leapt over fences.

I was scared
senseless
when six Rebs
entered
the cemetery,
and Mama fainted
among
the graves.

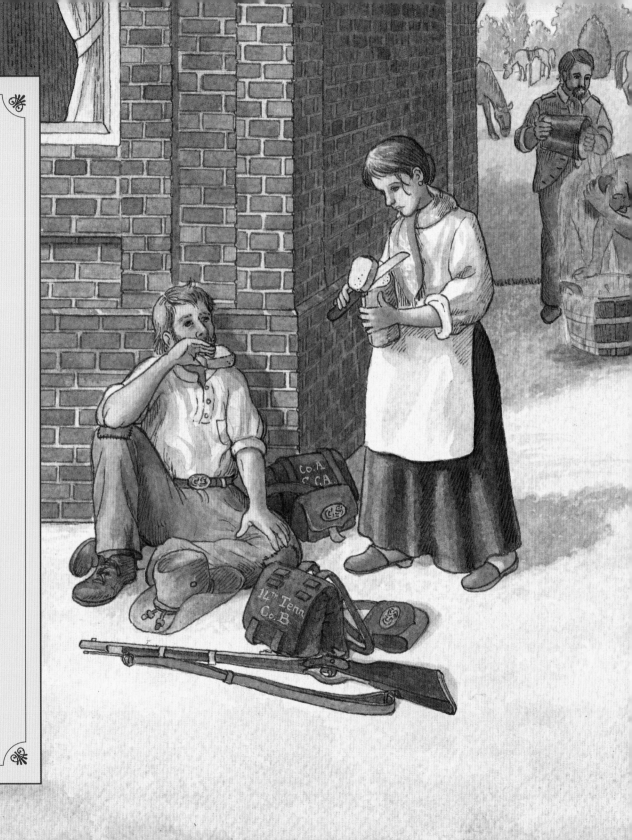

I ran to Mama
and sat her up,
giving her a sip
from a cup
of water.

The Rebs
begged for bread,
butter,
and milk.
I shook
as Mama took
a butcher knife
and sliced
hot bread
for them.

I fetched
glasses, tins,
cups,
and tubs,
and my brothers
pumped water
while I spread
fresh butter
on the bread
for the Rebs.

Poor George
and John
got blisters
on their hands
from the water pump,
but they insisted
on helping our mother
until the soldiers
were gone.

The Rebels
stole horses
all over town,
and they
burned down
the Rock Creek Bridge.

From the
cemetery's ridge,
we stared
in shock
as the railroad cars
crashed far
down
into the valley.

Mama's mouth
was a frown,
while thick smoke
darkened the sky
from July-blue
to a strange gray.

On Wednesday morning,
the first of July,
the Rebs
and their horses
arrived in full force,
and the battle
began.

Mama dropped
a cast-iron pan,
but she tried
to be brave,
until a shell
crashed
through
the window.

I cried,
thinking this could be
my last day
on earth.

There were cannons
on Cemetery Hill,
and it gave me chills
to know that
many soldiers
were dying.

We crept
down the steps
and into the
musty cellar,
fleeing
the Rebels' shells.

Huddling, shuddering
together,
we held hands
and begged God
to protect us,
and to let
this nightmare
end.

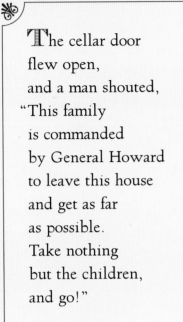

The cellar door
flew open,
and a man shouted,
"This family
is commanded
by General Howard
to leave this house
and get as far
as possible.
Take nothing
but the children,
and go!"

We ran fast
down the pike,
and a shell burst
right behind us.

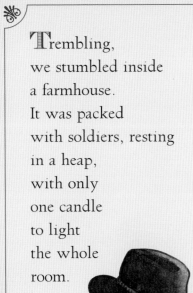

Trembling,
we stumbled inside
a farmhouse.
It was packed
with soldiers, resting
in a heap,
with only
one candle
to light
the whole
room.

One bleeding,
weeping soldier
motioned
to Mama,
and he showed
her a photo
of his young sons,
three boys
just like us.

The injured soldier
pleaded with Mama
for us to sleep
near him,
and we did,
while the man
wept.
He kept
begging God
to let
him live.

A few days later,
the battle ended,
and we headed home,
through the terrible mess
and stench.

Leaves were blown
from the trees,
and no birds chirped,
for they
had flown
away.

On the road,
we passed
the president
of the cemetery,
and he said
we had
a lot of work
to do.

"Three mean days," he said
as a tear creeped
down his cheek.
"I never dreamed
one town
could need
so many graves."

My eyes
were wide
at the first
sight
of our home.

Everything was
gone,
except for three
featherbeds,
full of
mud and blood.

There were fifteen
dead horses
before our door
and broken glass
in the grass.

Turning dirt,
working
the earth,
shoveling
from sunup
in morning
to noon,
I boosted
Mama's spirits
by singing hymns.

We worked
for days
and days,
my mother
and grandfather
and me.

Some neighbors
came to assist,
but soon
had to go away
because they
became sick
from the smell.

I gritted my teeth
and lifted the spade.

We dug graves
for more than
a hundred soldiers.

The wet wormy dirt,
heavy as boulders,
hurt my arms
and shoulders,
but I was glad
to do my part:
turning earth
for the soldiers.

Autumn arrived,
and my mother
gave birth
to a daughter.

Papa came
home,
and he praised
Mama and me
for digging
so many
graves.

Our family
prayed
for the brave
souls
of the soldiers
now lying
in graves
by our
home.

It was November 19,
1863—
a day
I'd always
remember.

President
Lincoln came
on the train
to Gettysburg
to dedicate
a new cemetery.
He made
a speech,
which made people weep.

I held
Rosa
as my mother
met the President,
and it was
the best
moment
ever
for the cemetery keepers
of Gettysburg.

To the memory of Elizabeth and her brave boys—L.O.H.

To all children past and present whose lives are touched by war—L.F.F.

Text copyright © 2007 by Linda Oatman High
Illustrations copyright © 2007 by Laura Francesca Filippucci

First published in the United States of America in 2007 by Walker Publishing Company, Inc.
Distributed to the trade by Holtzbrinck Publishers

For information about permission to reproduce selections from this book, write to Permissions,
Walker & Company, 104 Fifth Avenue, New York, New York 10011

Library of Congress Cataloging-in-Publication Data
High, Linda Oatman.
The cemetery keepers of Gettysburg / Linda Oatman High; illustrations by Laura Francesca Filippucci.
p.   cm.
Summary: With his father, the caretaker of Gettysburg's Evergreen Cemetery, off fighting in the Union Army, Fred Thorn endures the three-day Battle of Gettysburg and then helps his mother and grandfather bury around one hundred soldiers.
ISBN-13: 978-0-8027-8094-2 • ISBN-10: 0-8027-8094-6 (hardcover)
ISBN-13: 978-0-8027-8095-9 • ISBN-10:0-8027-8095-4 (reinforced)
1. Gettysburg, Battle of, Gettysburg, Pa., 1863—Juvenile literature. [1.Gettysburg, Battle of, Gettysburg, Pa., 1863.
2. United States—History—Civil War, 1861–1865—Campaigns.] I. Filippucci, Laura, ill. II. Title.
E475.53.H535   2006973.7'349—dc21   2006010194

The artist used watercolor on Arches paper and refining in brown ink to create the illustrations for this book.

Book design by Maura Fadden Rosenthal/Mspace

Visit Walker & Company's Web site at www.walkeryoungreaders.com

Printed in China
2 4 6 8 10 9 7 5 3 1
All papers used by Walker & Company are natural, recyclable products
made from wood grown in well-managed forests. The manufacturing processes
conform to the environmental regulations of the country of origin.

AUTHOR'S NOTE

The cemetery keeper of Gettysburg's Evergreen Cemetery was a man named Peter Thorn, who was off serving with the Union army at the time of the Gettysburg battle. Peter's wife, Elizabeth Masser Thorn, became the caretaker of the cemetery during his absence. She lived in the gatehouse with her three sons—then ages seven, five, and three. After the three-day battle drew to a close, Elizabeth (with the help of her oldest son and her father) buried about one hundred soldiers. She was paid just thirteen dollars, her husband's salary for one month's work.

Three months after the battle, Elizabeth gave birth to a daughter. She suffered from poor health for a long time after the Battle of Gettysburg.

Elizabeth and Peter Thorn both died in 1907. They are buried together in Gettysburg's Evergreen Cemetery.

THE GETTYSBURG ADDRESS

FOUR SCORE AND SEVEN YEARS AGO our fathers brought forth on this continent, a new nation, conceived in Liberty, and dedicated to the proposition that all men are created equal. Now we are engaged in a great civil war, testing whether that nation, or any nation so conceived and so dedicated, can long endure. We are met on a great battlefield of that war. We have come to dedicate a portion of that field, as a final resting place for those who here gave their lives that that nation might live. It is altogether fitting and proper that we should do this. But, in a larger sense, we can not dedicate—we can not consecrate—we can not hallow—this ground. The brave men, living and dead, who struggled here, have consecrated it, far above our poor power to add or detract. The world will little note, nor long remember what we say here, but it can never forget what they did here. It is for us the living, rather, to be dedicated here to the unfinished work which they who fought here have thus far so nobly advanced. It is rather for us to be here dedicated to the great task remaining before us—that from these honored dead we take increased devotion to that cause for which they gave the last full measure of devotion—that we here highly resolve that these dead shall not have died in vain—that this nation, under God, shall have a new birth of freedom—and that government of the people, by the people, for the people, shall not perish from the earth.